"Angeles National Forest" is published by the Big Santa Anita Historical Society, a non-profit corporation whose officers and board of directors are individuals who have spent a good portion of their lives in the San Gabriel Mountains. These mountains have so influenced the lives of these individuals that contributing their time and talents to the society is their way of putting something back.

"Angeles National Forest" is the sixth book published by the Big Santa Anita Historical Society since its inception in 1981. Funds from the sale of these books are used to carry on the society's work, "Preservation Through Education," and to support various projects in the Angeles National Forest.

Color photography by Roy Murphy

Black and white photos from John W. Robinson collection

Design and production by Roy Murphy

Color separations by Select Color, Inc.

Printed by Pace Lithographers, Inc.

Copyright © 1991 by Big Santa Anita Historical Society

Printed in U.S.A.

ISBN 0-9615421-4-4

Published by the Big Santa Anita Historical Society
"Preservation Through Education"

7 North Fifth Ave., Arcadia, CA 91006

Previous page: North face of Mt. Baldy from Blue Ridge, here bright with guard lupine whose leaves wear "fur coats," a dense matting that protects them from alpine cold.

Top: Merriam's chipmunks are lively and engaging little neighbors in the higher elevations of the forest.

Above: A young bighorn explores its rocky world.

ANGELES NATIONAL FOREST

CONTENTS

Sugar pine and white fir frame Mt. Baldy, the highest peak (10,064') in Angeles National Forest. Clouds fill the deep gorge separating it from South Mt. Hawkins.

Crystal Lake is natural; it is fed by runoff and springs located on landslides that partly enclose its basin.

9

INTRODUCTION

My introduction to Angeles National Forest took place on a wintry day in the 1940s when I was barely eight years old. With snow-play in mind, Dad decided he'd fill our old Chevy with family and a few friends from the neighborhood, L.A.'s Silverlake District, and head for Angeles Crest Highway. I have vivid memories of peering through the ice-cold windows for my first glimpse of the white stuff. On that trip, and usually on the ones that followed through the years, we'd spot it as we neared the highway's Mount Wilson cutoff. But the snow often lay several miles up the road at Chilao or Mount Waterman, and the time between sighting and stopping seemed like eternity. Excitement would build to the point where, when Dad finally pulled to the side of the road, the rest of us flew out the doors before the engine even stopped turning over.

Since then, the forest has become one of my best friends, always there in time of need, candid about her imperfections, eager to bring forth a smile with her moods; strong, silent and reassuring in her ability to humble and renew me with her seemingly timeless abundance of life. Cities are places where people communicate with each other. Wilderness is for people to commune with their own souls.

During my lifetime, urban growth has brought many urban problems to the City of Los Angeles and surrounding suburbs. The Silverlake streets where I used to play so freely today have become an inner city danger zone, towns once separated by open fields and farmland now stretch endlessly across the basins and valleys to form the sprawling Los Angeles Metropolitan Area.

In contrast, Angeles National Forest is still basically the same forest I knew as a child. True, there are more people in some places, but walk a mile or two from parking and you are alone, a part of the ever changing world of nature.

Angeles National Forest is the sixth book published by the Big Santa Anita Historical Society. I wish it had been the first but we had some growing to do.

Elna Bakker, Roy Murphy and John Robinson have spent the greater part of their lives studying the mountains that rim the Los Angeles area. They are all professionals in their field, the forest. It is my hope that the knowledge they share in the pages that follow will spark a desire within you to search toward a greater understanding of your forest.

Opposite: Incense cedar and ponderosa (yellow) pine flourish around Big Cienega Springs on the road to South Mt. Hawkins.

ISLAND IN THE SKY — THE GEOLOGY, PLANTS AND WILDLIFE OF ANGELES NATIONAL FOREST

Greater Los Angeles is the single major urban area in the country that not only is cut in two by one mountain range, the Santa Monicas, but is backed by another, the San Gabriels. Commanding the northern skyline like a fortress guarding the valleys below, the San Gabriel Mountains form the centerpiece of the east-west trending Transverse Ranges. Stubbornly resistant to the north-south topographical "grain" typical of much of the North American continent, this transverse system stretches through southern California from mountains north of Indio in the desert to the east, westward to the mountains lining the coast in Santa Barbara County.

Angeles National Forest was established to protect not only most of the San Gabriel Mountains, but the rugged back country north of the Antelope Valley Freeway which this introductory guidebook refers to as the Castaic Mountains, after place names commonly used in the area. Covering roughly one-fourth of Los Angeles County, Angeles National Forest extends from the San Bernardino county line on the east to the Ventura county line, just west of Interstate 5.

Though roughly a third of the size of Los Padres National Forest, its sister to the west, Angeles National Forest includes truly remarkable terrain. More diverse in age and rock type than the Sierra Nevada, the San Gabriel and Castaic mountains are some of the most geologically complex ranges in the country. They also claim a unique assortment of natural systems. Twenty-two different ecosystems have been described for the area, many more than those of the Cascade Mountains of Washington.

The San Gabriel Mountains are separated lengthwise into a steeply rugged southern front and a taller northern bulwark by a string of east-west trending canyons. Carved out along the San Gabriel fault, once the main trace of the San Andreas fault, they include the east and west forks of the San Gabriel River. Numerous other canyons have been hewn out of the flanks of the range, encircling it like the spokes of a wheel. A main cluster of peaks rises well over 9,000 feet. Interlocked with other summits in an alpine backbone, Mount San Antonio (Mount Baldy) and Mount Baden-Powell dominate the northern slope.

The Castaic Mountains are triangular in shape, the apex being where the Antelope Valley Freeway meets Interstate 5. Three high ridges command the northern slope—westernmost Liebre Mountain, Sawmill Mountain in the middle and tall enough for timber, and to the east, Sierra Pelona. Bounded on the north by valleys formed along the San Andreas fault, the country south of them is extremely crumpled and cut by several northeast-southwest trending canyons including San Francisquito, Bouquet and Mint.

Looking up at their massive flanks, it is difficult to believe that the San Gabriel and Castaic mountains have been in their present location for less than a million years, only an instant of geologic time. These are mountains on the move. Not only are they being heaved up by motion on reverse faults along their southern bases, they are migrating to the northwest. The mighty San Andreas fault is responsible for the motion that ultimately will carry the San Gabriel and Castaic mountains as far north as Alaska! The average rate of movement is about two inches a year, and much of the actual motion is accomplished by earthquakes, some of great magnitude, on the San Andreas and related faults.

The ranges are complicated welters of rocks, varying in age from

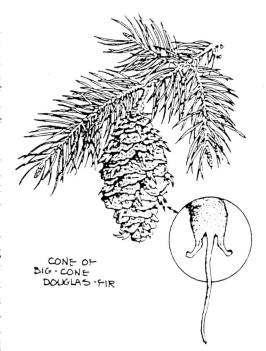

CONE OF BIG-CONE DOUGLAS-FIR

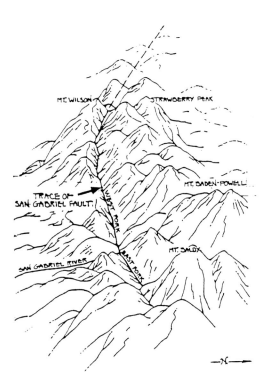

AERIAL VIEW OF THE SAN GABRIEL MOUNTAINS

Illustrations by Pat Brame

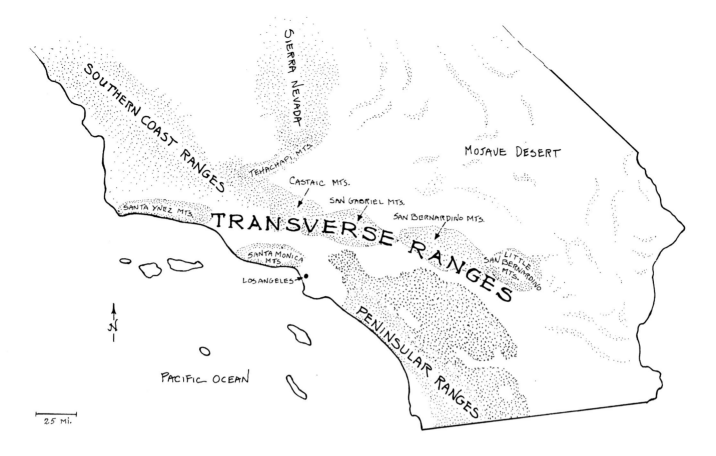

Map labels: SOUTHERN COAST RANGES · SIERRA NEVADA · MOJAVE DESERT · TEHACHAPI MTS · CASTAIC MTS. · SAN GABRIEL MTS. · SAN BERNARDINO MTS. · SANTA YNEZ MTS. · TRANSVERSE RANGES · LITTLE SAN BERNARDINO MTS. · SANTA MONICA MTS · LOS ANGELES · PENINSULAR RANGES · N · PACIFIC OCEAN · 25 Mi.

1.7 billion years to piles of debris deposited during last winter's storms. It may help to think of them as part of a giant "sandwich" that was put together tens of millions of years ago near the present California-Mexico border, some 186 miles south of where the range is today.

The upper slice of the "sandwich" is a collection of various types of continental crust. Some of the rocks have been greatly changed (metamorphosed), and it is difficult to tell what they were originally. Others are plutonic, formed when molten masses cooled slowly deep underground. One of these rock types (known technically as the anorthosite body) is particularly interesting because it is very ancient, over one billion years old, and also extremely rare in the western part of the continent (although it is common on the moon!)

By the end of the Dinosaur Age, about 66 million years ago, these huge chunks of crustal rocks were assembled on the western edge of the North American continent. At the same time the lower slice of the "sandwich," a slab of ocean floor, was slowly moving towards North America and in time began thrust-ing beneath the western edge of the continent. The two slices then settled into place, one on top of the other, and waited for the next great event, the formation of the San Andreas fault.

About thirty million years ago two enormous chunks of the earth's crust began sliding past each other. The piece of crust west of the San Andreas fault is advancing to the northwest, past the North American continental plate (see diagram on page 14). As new geologic forces took over, the land surface in the vicinity of the "sandwich" began breaking up, forming basins and uplands. Rubble eroding from higher ground filled the valley floors, piling up layers of mud, sand and other debris that hardened into the sedimentary beds now encircling much of this mountainous country. Such rocks line either side of Interstate 5 from where it leaves the San Fernando Valley to Gorman, some forty miles to the north. Those exposed in the western edge of the Castaic Mountains, near Pyramid Lake, are part of an ancient basin floor that contains one of the most detailed and complete geologic records of this period in California.

Finally the "sandwich" was cut in half by the developing San Andreas fault system. One part remained in place east of the Salton Sea where rocks of both slices are now exposed in nearby mountains. The other began a long journey. As the land west of the fault moved to the northwest, it carried with it the part of the "sandwich" that was to become the San Gabriel and Castaic mountains, moving them away from the Mexican border, past the San Bernardino Mountains and into the positions they now occupy. At the same time compression and other related geologic forces were at work, not only lifting the ranges to to their present heights but shattering their rocks to pieces.

Such processes sped up the work of erosion, which was, and still is, busy carving out steep-walled canyons. Erosion removes as much as seven tons of soil and rock from every acre of mountain slope each year. In pre-flood control times this debris was strewn out on the alluvial slopes slowly building at the mouths of the canyons draining the ranges. Wildfires periodically sweep through the mountains, destroying both the brushy cover

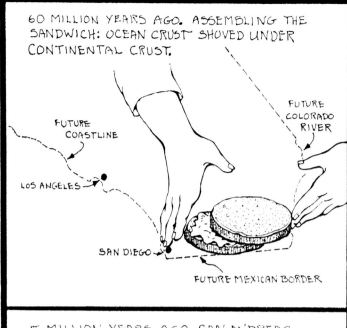

60 MILLION YEARS AGO. ASSEMBLING THE SANDWICH: OCEAN CRUST SHOVED UNDER CONTINENTAL CRUST.

FUTURE COLORADO RIVER

FUTURE COASTLINE

LOS ANGELES

SAN DIEGO

FUTURE MEXICAN BORDER

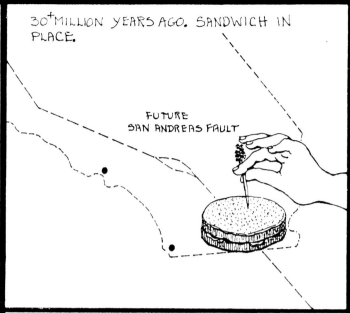

30+ MILLION YEARS AGO. SANDWICH IN PLACE.

FUTURE SAN ANDREAS FAULT

5 MILLION YEARS AGO. SAN ANDREAS FAULT BEGINS TO CUT THE SANDWICH IN TWO.

SAN ANDREAS FAULT

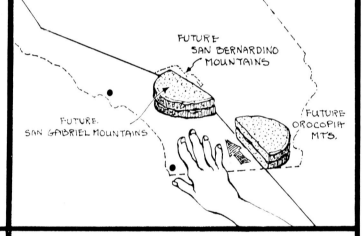

2 TO 3 MILLION YEARS AGO. LAND WEST OF THE SAN ANDREAS FAULT IS MOVING TO THE NORTHWEST, TAKING PART OF THE SANDWICH WITH IT.

FUTURE SAN BERNARDINO MOUNTAINS

FUTURE SAN GABRIEL MOUNTAINS

FUTURE OROCOPIA MTS.

A GEOLOGIC "DELI DELIGHT"

MILLIONS OF YEARS AGO THE ROCKS OF THE SAN GABRIEL MOUNTAINS WERE ASSEMBLED AS PART OF A GIANT "SANDWICH." SINCE THEN THESE ROCKS HAVE BEEN MOVED TO THE NORTHWEST AND THRUST UP TO THEIR PRESENT HEIGHT.

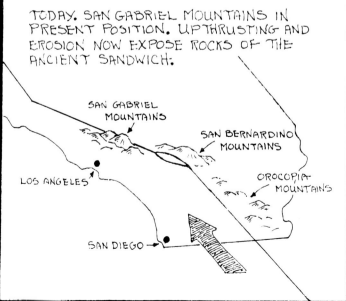

TODAY. SAN GABRIEL MOUNTAINS IN PRESENT POSITION. UPTHRUSTING AND EROSION NOW EXPOSE ROCKS OF THE ANCIENT SANDWICH.

SAN GABRIEL MOUNTAINS

SAN BERNARDINO MOUNTAINS

OROCOPIA MOUNTAINS

LOS ANGELES

SAN DIEGO

Illustrations by Pat Brame

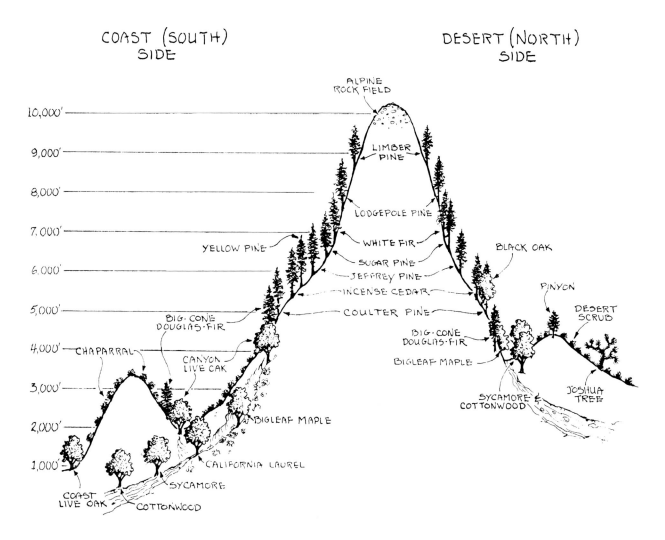

COAST (SOUTH) SIDE

DESERT (NORTH) SIDE

ALPINE ROCK FIELD

10,000'

9,000'

LIMBER PINE

8,000'

7,000'

LODGEPOLE PINE

WHITE FIR

YELLOW PINE

BLACK OAK

6,000'

SUGAR PINE

JEFFREY PINE

PINYON

INCENSE CEDAR

5,000'

COULTER PINE

DESERT SCRUB

BIG-CONE DOUGLAS-FIR

4,000' CHAPARRAL

BIG-CONE DOUGLAS-FIR

CANYON LIVE OAK

BIGLEAF MAPLE

3,000'

JOSHUA TREE

2,000'

BIGLEAF MAPLE

SYCAMORE & COTTONWOOD

CALIFORNIA LAUREL

1,000'

SYCAMORE

COAST LIVE OAK

COTTONWOOD

and trees of woodland and forest. They also expose broken surface rock and soil to further erosion. Landslides and debris flows are common occurrences, particularly during heavy storms.

Though torrential rains help unravel these unstable slopes, they are infrequent. Angeles National Forest is in a climatic region characterized by long dry summers and short wet winters. Several local variations alter this general pattern. Temperatures drop as altitude increases. Cold air is less able than warm air to hold moisture in vapor form. When the air is chilled sufficiently its vapor condenses, forming raindrops. Thus the cooler, higher ridges enjoy more precipitation than the foot of the range, and in winter it falls as snow. Most of this precipitation, however, is squeezed out of winter storms crossing over the mountains from the seaward side to the interior, and little moisture is left for the Mojave

Desert to the north. This rainshadow effect, as it is called, has played an important role in creating the deserts of the Southwest.

Plant life of Angeles National Forest is distributed accordingly. Drought-tolerant chaparral, an "elfin forest" of stiffly branched shrubs and small trees, occupies lower slopes in the southern side of the forest, giving way to even more water-conserving scrub growth on the desert side. About halfway up Mount Wilson, visitors to the forest begin to encounter big-cone Douglas-fir (often referred to as bigcone spruce), the characteristic cone-and-needle tree of lower elevations. This species, whose branches are draped with needle-covered twigs, resembles its close cousin, Douglas-fir. The cones of both have scales that are separated by bracts having an uncanny resemblance to the hindquarters of a mouse, two legs, tail and all! Digger pine, typical tree of the Sierra foot-

hills, continues as far south as Liebre and Sawmill mountains in the northern Castaics.

Big-cone Douglas-fir and digger pine give way to the typical cone-bearing trees of mid-elevations at about 5,000 feet, which, for the sake of comparison, is slightly lower than Mount Wilson. Jeffrey pine, which tolerates higher and drier conditions better than ponderosa pine, is distinguished from its near relative by the vanilla-like odor of its bark and larger, less prickly cone.

Coulter pine is another mid-elevation cone-bearer. It is common in the Chilao-Charlton Flat area and can be distinguished by its huge cones, the heaviest of all the pine species. Sugar pine, bearer of the world's longest cones, and incense cedar are also part of the mid-elevation forest. Both are plentiful in many places along Angeles Crest Highway, such as east of Chilao, while Icehouse Canyon and Buck-

horn Flat have fine concentrations of impressively large incense cedars. White fir joins the forest above 6,000 feet, particularly on cooler north-facing hillsides, and shares the higher slopes with groves of lodgepole pine. A notable stand of these resident pines of the high country occurs in Dorr Canyon between Dawson Saddle and Vincent Gap, where a number of them can be seen easily from the highway.

Only those who hike to such peaks as Mount Baden-Powell can become acquainted with the weather-beaten limber pines that are over a thousand years old and the alpine rock fields perched above them. For those who attempt such rigorous activity, the climb is well worth it. The views are fabulous, and the gnarled old fellows of timberline are delightful companions.

On the desert side Joshua trees and one-needled pinyons mark the transition between the cone-bearing trees of higher altitude and the scrub growth below. Visitors to Devil's Punchbowl County Park, just south of Pearblossom, meet these interesting species of small desert trees while approaching from the north.

Where water is more abundant such as in Big Santa Anita and other canyons or on sun-scarce north-facing slopes, the vegetation becomes more luxuriant. California bay (laurel) and coast and canyon live oaks create shady woodlands sheltering columbine, Humboldt lilies and other moisture-needing wildflowers. Black oak is one of three deciduous oaks in Angeles National Forest. In the San Gabriels it is restricted to the north side of Blue Ridge (Wrightwood west to Jackson Lake), but it is common on Liebre Mountain and other neighboring ridges of the Castaic Mountains. Though particularly pleasing in summer with its richly green foliage, black oak adds lively notes of autumn color as do alders, willows, sycamores, big-leaf maples, cottonwoods and other trees typical of stream banks and canyon floors.

The two remaining deciduous oaks that live in Angeles National Forest are valley oak, one of the stateliest of American oaks, and blue oak. Both occur in the northern part of the Castaic Mountains, making use of water trapped at or near the surface along the San Andreas fault system. Valley oak also grows in the Newhall area.

The plant distribution just described for Angeles National Forest is typical of mountainous areas in dry climates. They are islands of tree growth fringed by various types of scrubby vegetation at lower elevations. Though this national forest has fewer tree species than the forests of the western slope of the Sierra Nevada, where the annual rainfall is much greater, it is a tenacious assortment, "hanging in there" as the climate became warmer and drier at the end of the Ice Age.

Wildlife is abundant in many parts of Angeles National Forest. Spread out a picnic supper under the oaks at Chantry Flats on a mellow summer evening. You may soon be sharing your place with some engaging members of a California ground squirrel family or a noisily demanding scrub jay. Just as vocal, red-capped and black-shawled acorn woodpeckers swoop through the oak branches in dra-

Top: Flowering orange-red, heart-leaved penstemons thrive in nutrious ash left by a brushfire.

Above: Over a billion years old, Mendenhall gneiss is exposed in road cuts on both sides of the Upper Tujunga Canyon Road just below its intersection with the Angeles Crest Highway.

Opposite: Contorted by alpine winds, some of the limber pines of Mt. Baden-Powell are over a thousand years old.

Top left: Oak grove-dwelling acorn woodpeckers share stored food, nestling care and other responsibilities of communal life.

Top right: Bobcats flourish in many parts of Angeles National Forest.

Middle left: The adaptable coyote, now at home in many environments including city suburbs.

Middle right: Plumy-tailed grey squirrels share woodland and forest with many seed-eating animals.

Lower right: Can you find the fence lizard? Its scaly skin blends with the tree bark.

Bottom right: Swallowtail butterfly searching for nectar in a wallflower.

matic trajectories. Red-tailed hawks high overhead keep wary eyes out for ground squirrels while great horned owls will soon be hunting for woodrats and other rodents now beginning to emerge from their daytime retreats. From across the canyon the first high call of a coyote announces its intention to begin the evening's hunt. On the opposite ridge a mule deer and her fawn work through the undergrowth for suitable shelter, while down in the moist canyon bottom, newts and other salamanders are winding down the day's business.

Much closer, red harvester ants may take exception to your presence, but more hospitable insects such as gall wasps are only interested in finding homes for their larvae on twigs and leaves of nearby oak trees and shrubs. Western fence lizards are seeking the last warmth of the sun on rocks not too far away, though a more secretive California kingsnake may not be anxious to disclose itself. Most of the creatures of Angeles National Forest go about their activities unobserved by human visitors. There are the fortunate few, however, who glimpse bighorn sheep, bobcats, gray foxes and even mountain lions, black bears and the ever-elusive ringtail cat, attractive little cousin of the raccoon also common in many places in the region.

Angeles National Forest is many things to many people. It may be the challenge of an unexplored mountain trail, a haven of needle-scented cool breeze above the smoggy heat of the lowland summer, or in winter a snow-quilted playground. Enjoy! And remember to leave only footprints and take only memories.

Top: Here hidden by shoreline rocks, Pyramid Lake attracts a great blue heron.

Above: To the left the 60 foot and 150 foot solar tower telescopes and the 60 inch and 100 inch dome telescopes of the famed Mt. Wilson Observatory. Television towers for all Los Angeles stations rise in the background.

Upper Tujunga
Chaparral yuccas and snow are not uncommon companions. These spike-leafed plants occur as high as 8,000 feet.

Twin Peaks
Moist air masses from south and east visit Angeles National Forest in summer, piling into thunderheads that may bring appreciated rain.

Cloudburst Summit
Weathering has attacked this outcrop, wearing away the rock surfaces exposed in parallel joints, or cracks.

Jeffrey pines rise above late-blooming rabbitbrush and California fuchsia on Lightning Ridge.

Winter's chill winds have twisted this Jeffrey pine into a natural bonsai.

Limber pines on the summit of Mt. Baden-Powell overlook the Mojave Desert.

Overleaf: Winter-red toyon berries brighten the foreground while South Mt. Hawkins broods under a cloudy cover.

23

THE SAGA OF THE MOUNTAINS

Angeles National Forest encompasses fully a fourth of Los Angeles County, extending from Pyramid Lake, near the Ridge Route, eastward across the San Gabriel Mountains to Mount Baldy. This wrinkled mountain country to the north and northwest of the Los Angeles basin has a rich heritage of human use. Lying close to a major population center, the forest has been utilized for its mineral and timber resources, for grazing, for water, and for recreation to a degree equalled by few other national forests in the nation.

First to use the mountains were Indian peoples of Shoshonean stock — Gabrielinos (to use the Spanish name for them) in the southern foothills, Fernandeños in the western canyons, and Serranos in the eastern and northern parts of the forest. Although their homes, usually brush huts or wickiups were generally below the foothills, these peoples depended heavily on the mountains for food, water and materials for tools and weapons. They made annual summer pilgrimages to hunt deer and rabbit and to gather acorns and pine nuts. Chaparral was an abundant source of many necessities. Manzanita berries were pressed for cider, and the leaves were smoked. Greesewood provided arrow shafts for hunting. Yucca fibers were used to make nets and ropes. Wild berries were picked and consumed as a delicacy.

The coming of the Spaniards changed life in the pleasant valleys below the mountains forever. In 1771, along the grassy banks of the Rio Hondo, Mission San Gabriel Arcangel was founded, and soon thereafter the Gabrielinos were incorporated into the mission community. Mission San Fernando Rey de España, founded in 1797, became the home of the less-numerous Fernandeños. At the height of mission activity — around 1806 these two outposts of the cross numbered some 2,000 Indians in their widespread flocks.

Several decades later came the era of the great land grant ranchos, bringing a pastoral way of life to the valleys. These spacious cattle ranches that nudged against the south slopes of the mountains bore the familiar names of San Fernando, Tujunga, La Cañada, San Pascual, Santa Anita, Azusa de Duarte, and San Jose.

The Spanish and Mexican Californios used the mountains very little except as a source of water. Vaqueros often rounded up stray cattle in the canyons. When there were buildings to be constructed, woodcutters sometimes took timber from the lower canyons. Grizzly bears, numerous in the mountains then, were stalked, lassoed and captured, then dragged to the bull ring in El Pueblo de Los Angeles to be sacrificed in brutal bear-bull contests.

Although the Spaniards failed to penetrate into the hidden heart of the range, they did give the mountains their name — two names, in fact, that have existed side by side down to recent years. Diarists for the Anza Expedition of 1775-1776 refer to the mountains north of the Los Angeles basin as "Sierra Madre" (Mother Range). Fray Francisco Garces, the missionary-explorer who journeyed on both sides of the range in 1776, used the term "Sierra de San Gabriel" in his diary. Both "Sierra Madre" and "San Gabriel" were in common usage until 1927, when the United States Board on Geographic Names finally ruled in favor of the latter. Today, "San Gabriel Mountains" is universally accepted.

With the coming of the Anglos in the 1840s, the San Gabriels began to receive more attention. Prospectors, hunters, bandits, and later homesteaders and squatters were the pioneers in unveiling the secrets of the mountains. These hardy individuals first entered the wooded canyons, then forged their way over the ridges into the high country — terrain the rancheros had scorned.

Stories of gold in the San Gabriels go back as far as the 1790s, when the fabled "Lost Padres" mine was supposedly worked by the mission fathers and their Indian neophytes from San Fernando Mission. But the earliest verified gold mining — not only in the San Gabriels but in all of California — occurred after Francisco Lopez discovered gold clinging to the roots of some wild onions in Placerita Canyon, just west of present-day Santa Clarita, in 1842. The San Fernando Placers, as the discovery was called, were worked on and off for about a decade, until strikes elsewhere drew the miners away. By far the largest gold strike in the San Gabriels occurred on the East Fork of the San Gabriel River. The precious metal was discovered in the canyon gravels in 1854, and for the next eight years the East Fork was the scene of frenzied activity, with gold pans, sluice boxes and long toms being utilized on a grand scale. The boom ended with startling abruptness when heavy rains caused a flood to surge down the canyon, totally obliterating the mining camp of Eldoradoville and all the miners' works, in 1862. Mining continued in the East Fork into recent years, but never again on the scale of the early boom days. Gold recovery on a lesser scale also occurred in Big Tujunga Canyon, on Mount Gleason, along Lytle Creek, and in the Liebre country to the northwest.

Bandits, including Jack Powers, Salmon Pico, Juan Flores, and the legendary Tiburcio Vasquez turned to the San Gabriels for refuge. They drove stolen cattle and horses up the canyons and pastured them in the back country flats, particularly in the Chilao-Horse Flats area. Utilizing

Switzer's Camp CA 1886. Commodore Perry Switzer on left.
This was the first trail resort in the San Gabriel Mountains.

a faint network of old Indian trails, these outlaws established isolated hideouts deep in the mountains.

The pioneer trail-builder in the San Gabriels was Benjamin Wilson, owner of Rancho San Pascual, who in 1864 reworked an old Indian path up Little Santa Anita Canyon to the top of the mountain that now bears his name. During the next three decades, trails were blazed up all the major canyons of the front range, some of them continuing over the ridges and into the back country. In increasing numbers, homesteaders and squatters followed these trails and found favorite spots on which to build their cabins. The names of many of these early mountain men have come down to the present, attached to canyons, camps, and peaks – Henninger, Millard, Switzer, Sturtevant, Newcomb, Chantry, Chilao, Islip, Dawson, Vincent, Manker, to name a few.

Coldbrook stage crossing San Gabriel River.

Hydraulic mining at Baldy Notch, 1895.

Almost all of these pioneers came into the mountains for economic reasons — to mine gold, to cut timber, to pasture livestock, to establish a home. Around 1885 a new reason for going to the mountains arose — recreation. Great numbers of San Gabriel Valley residents journeyed up Benjamin Wilson's trail to camp among the pines and cedars and enjoy a panorama stretching from Pasadena farms and orchards to the sea. Equal numbers of Pomona Valley citizens scrambled over the Hogsback to enjoy a few days of camping and hunting in San Antonio Canyon. Azusa residents, as well as sportsmen from all over Southern California, travelled into San Gabriel Canyon to fish in the fabulous trout-filled waters of the San Gabriel River's three forks. Entrepreneurs took advantage of growing public interest in the mountains to establish trail resorts. Switzer's Camp in the Arroyo Seco, Strain's Camp on Mount Wilson, Martin's Camp on the Mt. Wilson-Mt. Harvard saddle, Sturtevant's Camp near the head of Big Santa Anita Canyon, Follows Camp and Camp Rincon in San Gabriel Canyon, and Dell's Camp in San Antonio Canyon were all booming mountain hostelries before the turn of the century. Thrill-seeking sportsmen ventured beyond the resorts, into the hidden heart of the mountains, to hunt grizzly bear, bighorn sheep and deer, plentiful in the early days.

Other people entered the mountains for a different reason — exploitation. Most 19th century Americans assumed that our natural resources were inexhaustable and therefore there was no need to conserve them. Sheep by the thousands were herded into the high country to devour every blade of grass, reducing mountain meadows to dust. Fires, many of them deliberately set by shepherds seeking more open grassland for their flocks, raged unchecked for days. Streams were polluted by unrestrained livestock use. Indiscriminate timber cutting to fuel Southern California's thriving building industry appeared imminent.

Fortunately, some far-sighted citizens of Los Angeles and the San Gabriel Valley became alarmed at this devastation of the mountain watershed and the effect that unrestrained exploitation would have on the precious water that nourished Southern California farms and orchards. One of these concerned citizens was Abbott Kinney, a rancher and land developer who lived at his Kinneloa Ranch above Altadena. Kinney is best remembered as the creator of Venice, the Southern California beach town that once had canals for streets, but it was as chairman of California's first Board of Forestry that he did his most important work. In the first report of the Board to Governor Stoneman in 1886, Kinney urged the "intelligent supervision of the forest and brush lands of California, with a view to their preservation." This California movement for forest conservation, sparked by Kinney and others, soon became part of a national movement. John Muir, using his eloquence in a series of magazine articles urging forest preservation, was the leading spokesman.

Ranger station at Pine Flat (now Charlton Flat), built in 1902.

28

Mt. Lowe Scenic Railway. Car crossing Grand Circular Bridge, 1895.

Congress finally responded by passing the Forest Reserve Act of 1891, granting the president authority "to set aside as public reservations public lands bearing forest wholly or in part covered with timber or undergrowth." As a result of this act, and strong pressure from Southern California civic leaders, President Benjamin Harrison signed the bill establishing the San Gabriel Timberland Reserve on December 20, 1892. This was the first forest reserve in California, and the eighth in the United States. The designation was at first rather ineffectual; there were no forest rangers assigned to protect the reserve until 1898. But gradually the San Gabriel Forest Reserve ("Timberland" was changed to "Forest" in 1893) was brought under efficient federal management and protection. In 1907 the name was changed to "San Gabriel National Forest," and the following year it became what we know today — "Angeles National Forest." A succession of capable supervisors — B.F. Allen, Rushton Charlton, Theodore Lukens, William Mendenhall, Sim Jarvi, William Dresser, and George Roby — have made the Angeles one of the most efficiently run national forests in America.

Worldwide fame came to the San Gabriels in the 1890s with construction of the Mt. Lowe Scenic Railway, considered one of the engineering wonders of its time. This breathtaking cable incline and mountainside trolley ride, along with associated hotels in Rubio Canyon, atop Echo Mountain, and at Crystal Springs on the south slope of Mt. Lowe, was the brainchild of inventor Thaddeus Lowe and engineer David Macpherson. The famed mountain railway-resort complex attracted over three million visitors between its start in 1893 until its abandonment, after the burning of Mt. Lowe Tavern, in 1936.

Man's quest for scientific knowledge played its part in the story of the mountains, too. In the days before city lights and air pollution interfered with sky-viewing, Mt. Wilson's broad summit was ideal for astronomical observation. The first telescope on Mt. Wilson was the 13-incher of the Harvard University Observatory, erected on the summit in 1889 (but removed the following year). 1904 saw the beginning of the Carnegie Institution's famed Mt. Wilson Observatory, one of the early 20th century's great scientific ventures. Largely through the initiative and enthusiasm of astronomer George Ellery Hale, several major instruments were placed on the mountain-top, the most important being the 60-inch reflector (1908), the 150-foot solar tower telescope (1912), and the 100-inch Hooker reflector (1917), the latter the world's largest optical telescope until the opening of the Mt. Palomar Observatory, with its mammoth 200-inch reflector, in 1948. In 1989, the Mt. Wilson Observatory was taken over by the Pasadena-based Mt. Wilson Institute.

Before highways crisscrossed the San Gabriels, the mountains were the delight of hikers. During the period from about 1895 to 1938 there occurred what historians call the Great Hiking Era. Multitudes of lowland residents enjoyed their weekends and holidays rambling over the range. Trails into the high country vibrated to the busy tramp of boots and the merry singing of hikers. The mountains were a local frontier for exploration and a challenge to the hardy. For some, hiking was simply a favorite sport; for others, it was almost a religion. Thousands rode the "Big Red Cars" (Pacific Electric trolleys) to the trailheads at Mt. Lowe, Sierra Madre, Azusa, and the mouth of San Antonio Canyon, donned knapsacks and headed into the canyons, many to continue far into the back country. Trail resorts sprang up to offer hospitality, food, and lodging to hikers. Such friendly haunts as Switzer's, Opid's, Sturtevant's, Roberts', Colby's, and, deep in the heart of the range, Loomis Ranch, were visited by a multitude every season.

A combination of disasters and encroaching civilization brought the Great Hiking Era to a close. The disasters were a series of fires and floods, the great destructive torrent of March 1938 being the final blow. Overnight, miles of canyon trails and cabins were obliterated. Civilization's encroachment took the form of paved highways, which relentlessly snaked their way into the heart of the mountains. The Angeles Crest Highway, begun in 1929, reached Red Box by 1934, Charlton Flat by 1937, and Chilao a year later. The Angeles Forest Highway across the range to Palmdale was completed in 1941. A new high-line highway up San Gabriel Canyon, built in the mid-1930s, allowed easy access to the East Fork and Crystal Lake country. Places that once lay a day or two of strenuous hiking away could now be reached in an hour or less of easy driving. One by one, the old trail resorts succumbed. As one old-timer sadly reflected, "Only people who hike for the love of hiking use these trails now."

Fortunately, the Forest Service, encouraged by conservation groups who fought to preserve some of our wilderness heritage from civilization's relentless march, set aside the San Gabriel and Cucamonga Primitive Areas in 1931. These became federally-protected wildernesses through the passage of the Wilderness Act of 1964. The Sheep Mountain Wilderness, surrounding the headwaters of the East Fork, was set aside in 1984.

In recent years, great numbers of people have visited Angeles National Forest, the vast majority by automobile. In 1945, Angeles visitors numbered an estimated 1,310,000. In 1987 the figure had swollen to more than 32,000,000, making the Forest one of the two or three most heavily visited in the nation. Another "Great Hiking Era" seems to be unfolding, as more and more lowland residents seek release from urban pressures by walking the mountain trails on weekends. Bicyclists in increasing numbers chug up the Angeles Crest Highway, then coast back down. Forest campgrounds are filled on weekends and holidays. In winter, skiers enjoy the snow-covered slopes at Mountain High, Mt. Waterman, and Kratka Ridge. Angeles National Forest is truly a recreational jewel, as well as an important watershed, to Southern California's huge population.

Enroute to Mount Wilson, CA 1906.

Top: Male California newts are rough-skinned and land-dwelling in summer. While breeding in the wet season they are smooth-skinned and aquatic.

Bottom left: Pacific rattlesnakes are more interested in avoiding visitors than attacking them.

Above: The pygmy owl is less nocturnal than others of its kind. It often hunts in daylight hours.

Overleaf: Big-leaf maple, here in fall color, and alder are water-spenders, growing only along streams and in other moist places.

Snow-frosted by a winter storm, a lone Jeffrey pine on Blue Ridge bends with the prevailing wind.

*Bright red lichen helps build soil on a barren outcrop,
preparing a suitable habitat for moss, ferns and
other plants.*

*Opposite: During heavy storms tons of rocky rubble
are carried downstream by the usually placid San
Antonio Creek.*

PHOTOGRAPHING
THE SAN GABRIELS

For more than 30 years the San Gabriels have captivated me as a photographer. California's High Sierras may offer more visual drama, but it is the subtlety of the San Gabriels that excites me. Because they are a semi-desert range, they abound in pastel tones. And since, unlike the Sierras, they are an east-west range, the cross-lighting is superb, with definition especially heightened in the early morning and late afternoon.

The dawn hours are my favorite time for photographing these mountains because the morning air is pure and still. Most of my camerawork is done with a tripod: For overall sharpness I like small aperture settings, which in turn require slower shutter speeds. Under those circumstances, even a slight breeze can cause enough movement in a tree or flower to ruin the picture, and breezes invariably begin stirring by the middle of the morning. An added drawback to shooting later in the day is haze.

While flowers make their appearance mostly in the spring, you can always find something blooming in the San Gabriels. No matter what season, their slopes are dotted with delicate details rich in color. Even in the driest years, I have found chamise, ceanothus, monkeyflower, paintbrush, bush lupine and prickly phlox in abundance. The Glendora Mountain Road seems to be a dependable source of such close-up detail as well as great views of the high country.

The mountainsides and canyons of the Angeles National Forest offer a surprising amount of fall color, particularly at Big Pines and Liebre Mountain. And winter can bring sparkling beauty to places that seem quite drab in summertime. For me, taking my cameras up into the high country after a fresh snow is the ultimate high. There, layers of clothing are preferred: before the sun comes up, or in the shade, it can be very cold; when the sun does come out, it grows quite warm.

Year-round, one of the biggest challenges in photographing these mountains is the sparseness of their vegetation. Rocky terrain reflects light with severity and can throw so much contrast into a scene that a pleasing photo is next to impossible. A cloudy day can be a fine photographic problem-solver in the San Gabriels. Or perhaps the solution may be to return to an appealing site when the sunlight will be reflecting differently off the surfaces, perhaps another time of day or even another time of year. In many instances, an imaginative photographer can use strong reflected light with good effect. Granite cliffs, for example, can bounce a wonderfully warm glow onto whatever stands opposite them. The San Gabriels shelter an abundance of wildlife to photograph. Deer, bighorn sheep and coyotes often can be seen along the Angeles Crest Highway, especially in the early morning. But the bobcats, cougars, bears, ringtailed cats and badgers that also inhabit the forests are more secretive. A good place to find a variety of birds is Chilao Visitor Center, where various woodpeckers, Steller's jays, scrub jays, Oregon juncoes, bandtail pigeons and mountain quail, to name just a few, congregate.

Through the years, I have come to rely on three cameras, all very rugged and most reliable—a prime requisite for outdoor photography. For most of my scenic work I use a Linhof 4×5 with the following lenses: 90 mm, 150 mm, 210mm, 12-inch Dagor, 360mm Apo-Roner. For details, flowers and wildlife I often use my Hasselblad 2 1/2 × 2 1/2 with 50mm, 150 mm and 350 mm lenses. Rounding out my equipment is a Nikon 35 mm FM2 camera body with 24mm, 35mm, and 70mm to 205mm and 50mm to 300mm zoom lenses.

I like the Linhof for its ruggedness, its long bellows extension, and front and back correction. The correction is needed for extreme depth of field and perspective adjustment. The large film size captures more critical detail. The Nikon gives me greater mobility, such as with some wildlife photography. The Hasselblad falls in between. Both the Hasselblad and the Nikon have motordrives for wildlife and remote setups.

By now, there is so much of these mountains in me and me in the mountains, that I must show them at their best. Like photographing an old friend, it's not enough to make a pretty picture. I must capture the mood and feeling in an intimate statement. I hope through my work I can help people to discover the real beauty of these great mountains, to experience their many moods and to enjoy our wonderful Angeles National Forest.

Opposite: At Lewis Falls, Soldier Creek cascades into a gorge carved out of rock weakened by geologic activity.

Looking east from Redbox, clouds gather over and in the canyon of the west fork of the San Gabriel River.

Opposite: Cold fronts from the north heap snow on Joshua trees in the desert foothills of the San Gabriels near Valyermo.

Early snow feeds a
stream that has built
an alluvial fan at the
base of Pine Mountain.
To the right a Jeffrey
pine dwarfs a late-
blooming rabbitbrush.

40

Above: Flat, grassy places such as Chilao Meadow are rare in the rugged San Gabriel Mountains.

Opposite: Tumbling down the streambed ground away the sharp corners of Soldier Creek's boulders.

Top: Glendora Ridge Road winds eastward, with Iron Mountain and Old Baldy dominating the skyline.

Bottom: Golden yarrow decorates a fallen log.

The Parish yucca, which grows only on the southern fronts of the San Gabriel and San Bernardino mountains is the tallest of four subtypes, reaching over 12 feet in height.

Near the summit of Liebre Mountain, the Pacific Crest Trail winds through a grove of autumn-bronzed black oaks.

Top left: Ponderosa pines near Big Cienega Springs. Slab-like plates of golden bark and prickly cones distinguish them from Jeffrey pines.

Above: Humboldt lilies prefer moist soils and shady places.

Left: A black bear cub takes a cautious peek at the world outside its sheltering tree.

Opposite: Willows and sycamores along the west fork of the San Gabriel River are kindled by an autumn afternoon sun.

Above: Hunting pairs of great horned owls keep in touch with two-toned hoots; the male's call is lower in pitch than the female's.

Top right: The mourning dove is the most common native dove in the United States.

Middle right: A white-breasted nuthatch is stretching away from the tree trunk in a pose unique to nuthatches.

Bottom right: Scrub jays are noisy and colorful brushland dwellers.

Opposite: Nature recycles fallen leaves, providing nutrients for these gooseberries and incense cedars.

Jackson Lake, a sag pond or water-filled depression, on the San Andreas fault.

Opposite: Looking northward from where the trail to Mt. Williamson meets the Angeles Crest Highway during a break in a winter storm.

Top left: Rime-frosted Jeffrey pines above the Angeles Crest Highway.

Top right: Early morning sun will melt the icy coating on a spray of toyon berries.

Bottom: Most of the black oaks in Angeles National Forest turn tawny shades of tan in fall, but a young tree on Liebre Mountain flaunts more vivid colors.

Sunny-flowered rabbitbrush signals the end of summer along the Angeles Crest Highway.

Top left: Purple nightshade is one of California's few native species of a plant family famous for both poison (datura) and food (potato, tomato).

Bottom left: Pink-flowered prickly phlox and yellow sticky monkeyflower form natural bouquets along the forest's highways.

Top right: Big-cone Douglas-fir, unlike its cousin Douglas-fir, is strictly a southern California species.

Bottom right: The big-leaf maple's catkins and new foliage are signs that spring is coming to Angeles National Forest.

Opposite: Ribbons of red bark carry water and food to the still-living parts of this manzanita. Staghorn lichen has invaded the dead branches.

Overleaf: High above the marine layer, mountain chaparral takes advantage of a sunny opening in the Jeffrey pine-white fir forest.

The crystalline rocks exposed on the northwest side of Strawberry Peak are granitic, once part of a molten mass deep inside the earth some 60 to 90 million years ago.

Opposite: Perched in a snow-covered white fir, a Clark's nutcracker surveys its snow-blanketed domain.

59

Sunrise gilds the crystalline rocks of Mt. Markham, one of a cluster of peaks northwest of Mt. Wilson.

Opposite: Mt. Baden-Powell's north and east slopes are home to lodgepole pine, one of the rarest cone-bearing trees in southern California.

Top left: Swarms of ladybugs preparing for winter hibernation.

Top right: The rare spotted owl is most at home in dense forests and oak thickets.

Middle right: A Clark's nutcracker perches on a newly-opened sugar pine cone.

Bottom right: The crests of Steller's jays distinguish them from scrub jays.

Opposite: Snow blankets the Pacific Crest Trail and Jeffrey pines at Cloudburst Summit.

A late-season storm has brought snow to the mountains behind Little Rock Lake.

Top: Sporting tall, slightly curving headplumes, a family of mountain quail forages for seeds and berries.

Bottom left: Like bears, raccoons relish anything from camping supplies to crayfish.

Bottom right: Speckled-coated mule deer fawns blend with the underbrush, camouflaging them from predators.

The rare Pierson's lupine is a floral bonanza along the Angeles Crest Highway east of Dawson Saddle.

Top right: Lemon lilies, also rare, are confined to moist, shady places.

Middle right: Lupine and mariposa lily complement each other's rosy hues.

Bottom right: Douglas wallflower blooms throughout Angeles National Forest.

Opposite: The crest of the San Gabriels from South Mt. Hawkins to Mt. Burnham forms an impressive backdrop as viewed from the Glendora Ridge Road.

Top left: Mountain lions are important in maintaining the balance of nature.

Middle left: Strong claws help the badger dig out its rodent prey.

Bottom left: Red-tailed hawks are common forest predators.

Top right: Ears up, a mule deer family is alert to possible disturbances.

Middle right: A red-shouldered hawk stands guard over its prey.

Bottom right: Many dark-eyed juncoes migrate to lower altitudes in winter.

Snow dusts the Angeles high country.

Top right: Depending on acorns and berries for food, band-tailed pigeons are common in both the woodlands and brushy areas of Angeles National Forest.

Above left: The brilliantly red snow plant, a member of the heather family, gets its food from decaying plant life.

Bottom right: A female rufous hummingbird in flight. These tiny birds seek nectar from early summer wildflowers.

Glory Hole, Pyramid Lake.

A FOREST FOR THE PEOPLE

As one of the 156 national forests in the United States, the Angeles has become nationally recognized as one of the few truly urban national forests. The Angeles receives heavy use by the people living in communities that closely surround the forest, people who need a place to escape from the pressures and frustrations of daily metropolitan or city living. Urban national forests present special challenges to the U.S. Forest Service because these forests receive different kinds of uses than the more traditional national forests located in more rural areas, great distances away from large population centers.

Between 1929 and 1960 federal, state and county governments financed the construction of scenic highways into the interior of the forest. The Angeles Crest Highway, the Angeles Forest Highway, San Gabriel Canyon Road and Big Tujunga Canyon Road all were built during this period, providing easy access to places that once required a day or two of strenuous hiking to reach.

But the Angeles essentially has experienced little change since presettlement times. Even today the forest can be a very wild and inhospitable place. Sudden storms can trap unprepared visitors without warning. People who wander off trails can become disoriented and lost in the rugged, chaparral-clad heart of the mountains. Steep, unstable terrain can cause falls and injuries.

Today this unique and picturesque 651,874 acre national forest comprises the single largest tract of publicly owned open space in Los Angeles County. The dense urbanization of southern California surrounds Angeles National Forest. Over seven million people live in Los Angeles County. Another thirteen million people live in adjacent counties. In the face of this overwhelming wave of humanity the Angeles continues even today to be the home of significant populations of trout, black bear, mountain lions, bighorn sheep, deer, coyotes, foxes, bobcats, hawks and a large variety of other birds, reptiles and mammals.

The metropolis that surrounds the forest has greatly complicated the management of this wildland ecosystem. First, the wildfires that continue to occur pose immediate threats to both life and property. These large, high intensity fires bring on the added risk of devastating floods that also threaten lives and cause widespread property damage. To simulate the natural process, forest managers use intentionally ignited fires called prescribed burns. These controlled blazes, set under strict conditions, allow nutrient-rich new vegetative growth necessary for wildlife. These prescribed burns also significantly reduce the impact that wildfires inflict on forest soils.

Second, the seven to eight million people who visit the forest every year view this rich, biologically diverse landscape as their extended backyard, a place to play and escape the frustrations of city life. Today's forest manager has the extremely delicate job of balancing these uses while maintaining and enhancing the plant and animal life chains that depend upon a healthy forest for their survival.

The national forests have a totally different purpose than national parks. "Park Rangers" manage the national parks under a basic philosophy of "preservation." Their guiding principle is to preserve the parks essentially in their wilderness state for present and future generations.

The Forest Service manages the national forests under the concept called multiple use management. This system allows for development but on an ecologically sound basis. Because of this, both present and future generations can expect visually pleasing, healthy, productive and biologically diverse ecosystems that contribute to the quality of life that most of us enjoy in southern California.

Residents and visitors to southern California unknowingly depend upon the Angeles for many of the natural resources that the forest provides. Although much of our water comes from other areas, water from our mountains provides a major share of the clean drinking water for nearby communities. This water is harnessed through a series of dams, debris structures and channels. These structures also protect the surrounding communities from floods caused by high intensity storms that occur every few years. How we manage the forest and these drainages, called watersheds, becomes the cornerstone for most of the multiple use decisions made by the Forest Service and cooperating federal, state and local agencies.

The Angeles is an often unappreciated national treasure. It has survived the first one hundred years of its existence because of the combined efforts of a number of highly dedicated Forest Service employees, permittees, concessionaires, a growing number of volunteer organizations and an involved public. We must all come to realize that the Angeles belongs to each of us. We need to appreciate it for what it is: a wild, beautiful, unique and biologically diverse landscape. A major part of our enjoyment involves learning enough about what makes ANGELES NATIONAL FOREST so special that we can treat it with the respect and care it deserves.

East of Vincent Gap.

ORIGIN OF SOME PLACE NAMES

Arroyo Seco: The name means "Dry Wash" in Spanish. It was given that name because the creek was dry when discovered by the Portolá Expedition in 1769.

Barley Flats: Named for the wild barley that once grew here. The flats were a favorite horse grazing area as early as the 1880s. Today Barley Flats is the site of a Los Angeles County detention camp.

Big Santa Anita Canyon: Rancho Santa Anita, below the canyon mouth, was granted to Hugo Reid in 1841 and was later owned by Lucky Baldwin. The prefix "Big" was added to distinguish it from its neighbor to the west, Little Santa Anita Canyon.

Big Tujunga Canyon: The derivation is unclear. The name comes from either *Tuxu'u,* Gabrielino word meaning "old woman," or *Ti'anga,* Southern Paiute for "mountain range."

Buckhorn: A favorite hunter's camp in the early days. The name derives from a pair of large antlers once nailed to a tree there.

Chantry Flats: Charlie Chantry, a Sierra Madre packer and jack-of-all-trades, filed for a special use permit here in 1907, ostensibly to build a cabin and put in an orchard. He never accomplished these objectives, but did graze his pack animals on the sloping flats for several years. The highway reached Chantry Flats in 1935.

Charlton Flats: Known as Pine Flat in the early days. Name was changed in the 1920s to honor Rush H. Charlton, Angeles Forest supervisor from 1906 to 1920 and from 1922 to 1925.

Chilao: The origin of this name is clothed in mystery. Legend says it was named for José Gonzales, a herder for the bandit Tiburcio Vasquez who allegedly knifed a bear and gained the nickname "Chileeyo," or "Hot Stuff." Another story says it was named for Chilao Silvas, who herded cattle here every summer for many years.

Crystal Lake: Judge Benjamin Eaton of Pasadena visited this little lake in 1887 and wrote: "The water is clear as a crystal and good to drink." This is the only natural lake in the San Gabriels. In years of draught it shrinks to little more than a small pond.

Eaton Canyon: Honors Pasadena Judge Benjamin Eaton, who piped water from the creek to his Fair Oaks ranch in the 1870s.

Follows Camp: Ralph Follows, an Englishman, founded a resort camp here on the San Gabriel's East Fork in 1891. For years it was one of the most popular hostelries in the mountains.

Hidden Springs: This small community along Mill Creek grew after the Angeles Forest Highway reached it in 1941. A flash flood in 1978 washed away many buildings and drowned ten persons.

Horse Flats: This campground near Chilao was once used to pasture and rebrand stolen horses.

Icehouse Canyon: Ice was cut here and stored in an icehouse for shipment to Los Angeles as early as 1858.

Mill Creek: This major tributary of Big Tujunga was the scene of gold mining excitement in the 1880s. The name derives from the small stamp mill of the Josephine Mine, on the east slope of the canyon.

Mount Baden-Powell: Known as North Baldy in the early days. Renamed for Lord R. S. Baden-Powell, British Army officer who founded the Boy Scouts in 1907. The Scouts long made annual pilgrimages to the peak.

Mount Lowe: Honors Thadeus S. C. Lowe, whose Mount Lowe Railroad climbed high on the south slope of the mountain in the years 1893 to 1936.

Mount San Antonio: Arroyo San Antonio is mentioned by diarists for the Anza expedition in 1774. Just when the name was extended from the canyon to the mountain peak is unknown. American settlers and miners, who loved to vulgarize place names, renamed it "Old Baldy." Today it is popularly known as Mount Baldy, but Mount San Antonio is the official name.

Mount Wilson: Benjamin Wilson, proprietor of the Lake Vineyard Ranch in today's San Marino, built a trail to the top in 1864 to obtain lumber for fences and wine barrels. For a brief period in 1889-90, and since 1904, Mount Wilson has been home to one of the world's major astronomical observatories.

Red Box: Named for a red fire tool box placed here by the Forest Service in the early 1900s.

Rincon: This small, shady nook just below the junction of the San Gabriel's West and North forks, was an Indian summer gathering and hunting camp long before the arrival of the white man. Charlie Smith turned Rincon into a popular camping and fishing resort in the early 1900s.

San Gabriel Canyon: Arroyo San Gabriel was the name bestowed on the creek that flowed near San Gabriel Mission in Spanish days. The San Gabriel's East Fork was the scene of a gold rush in the 1850s and early '60s. The canyon's waters were abundant with trout in the early years, when it was known as Azusa Canyon.

Sturtevant Falls, Camp: Wilbur Sturtevant established a popular resort camp here in upper Big Santa Anita Canyon in the 1890s.

Switzer Falls, Camp: Commodore Perry Switzer founded the first resort camp in the San Gabriels here in the upper Arroyo Seco, just above the falls, in 1884.

Vincent Gap: Named for Charles Tom Vincent, whose real name was Charles Vincent Daugherty, hunter and prospector who built a cabin near here in the 1870s. Vincent discovered the nearby Big Horn Mine in 1895.

Looking north from the junction of Big Tujunga Road and Angeles Forest Highway, snow-capped Mt. Gleason dominates the horizon.

Above left: Colorful masses of guard lupine grace the Angeles Crest Highway near the Sim Jarvi Memorial Vista.

Top right: The highly toxic datura is a member of the nightshade family.

Middle right: Prickly poppies are sunny-side up in the forest's drier areas.

Bottom right: Prickly pear cactus is common in the foothills.

Pyramid Lake as seen from lower Posey Canyon.

Left: Autumn-tinted bracken ferns enliven a shady canyon near Buckhorn.

Top right: California polypody ferns enjoy a shaded rocky crevice in Big Dalton Canyon.

Bottom right: Clumps of 5 foot tall paintbrush are often found near seeps and other damp places.

A spring-green morning invites a walk among the oaks of Big Dalton Canyon.

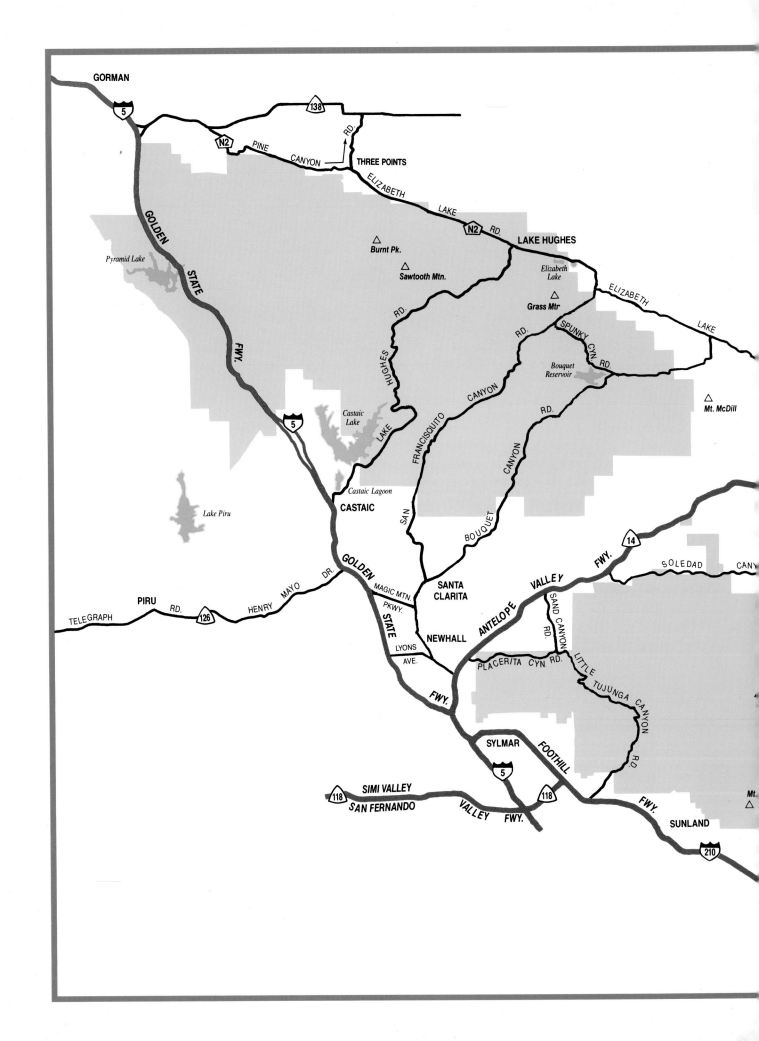